Fish for Lunch

By Sally Cowan

Ash met Pop at the dock.

"Let's get some fish!"
said Ash.

"Yum," said Pop.
"Fish for lunch!"

Pop and Ash had rods
and a net.

They sat at the end
of the dock.

Ash and Pop sat and sat.

Ash got up when she
got a tug on her rod!

"Pop! Check the fish
on my rod!" said Ash.

But it was much too little.
Ash had to toss it back.

Pop did not get a fish
at all!

"We did not have much
luck!" said Ash.

Shan's Shop

Let's get a fish
at Shan's shop!

Ash looked at boxes
and boxes of fish.

Pop put the fish
in a hot pan.

Ash got a big dish.

CHECKING FOR MEANING

1. What did Pop and Ash use to try to catch the fish? *(Literal)*

2. Where did they sit to catch the fish? *(Literal)*

3. Do you think Ash and Pop will go fishing again? Why? *(Inferential)*

EXTENDING VOCABULARY

fish	What is another word in the story that rhymes with *fish*? What is its meaning? If you take away the letter *f* at the start, what other letter can you put there to make a new word?
lunch	When do you have *lunch*? What do you have for lunch? Does everyone have the same food for lunch?
luck	What does *luck* mean? What is the difference between *good luck* and *bad luck*?

MOVING BEYOND THE TEXT

1. Other than rods and a net, what do you need
    to catch fish?

2. Why is it important to toss little fish back into
    the water?

3. What types of seafood do people eat other than fish?

4. What foods do people often eat with fish?

SPEED SOUNDS

sh	ch	th	th	ck	ng
		voiced	unvoiced		

PRACTICE WORDS

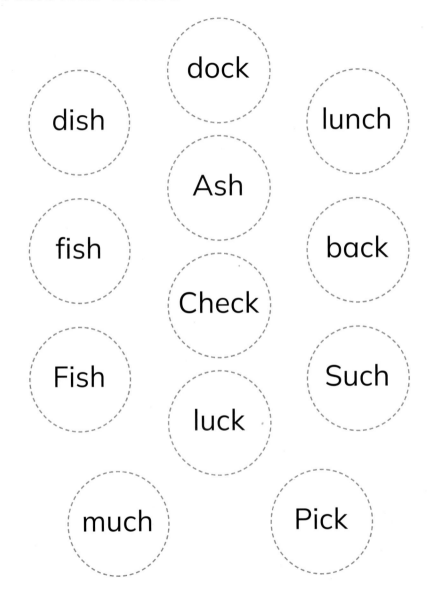

dock

dish

lunch

Ash

fish

back

Check

Fish

Such

luck

much

Pick